MY FIRST BOOK OF
MINDFULNESS

Enhance your child's social emotional health
through mindfulness, art and home experiments

by **Sunita Rai**, PsyD
With a Foreword by **Christopher Willard**, PsyD

mc **Marshall Cavendish**
Editions

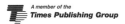

Contents

Acknowledgements

I am thankful to each and everyone of you who has inspired me to write. Yes, this includes you who have picked up this book. Without you, this would not have materialised.

My clients in my psychotherapy work had asked me years before to write on how to work with their children, especially in challenging times. Thank you for your suggestions and confidence in me. To the thousands of students whom I have lectured and supervised in your counselling and psychological work, thank you for nudging me numerous times to share my experience beyond the classroom. Your encouragement is invaluable. In fact, a lot of what I write here is based on my experience in the classrooms, workshops and in the therapy room.

To all my psychology, counselling, mindfulness, meditation and philosophy teachers, thank you for imparting your knowledge to me and your ever-flowing guidance. The fruit of your labour lies within these pages and beyond.

To Hernie Khames-Martin and Anya Sengupta, thank you for your creative artwork for this book. I remember sharing what I wanted to do in this book and my ideas for it and you both managed to seamlessly bring these ideas out in every one of the images. Thank you. This book is also dedicated to your hard and heart work.

Most importantly, I thank my parents, who were there for me. They were definitely not perfect and probably didn't know much of the strategies here, but they always tried their best to provide for all of their children. They had very little comforts, and so would always encourage us to study. Without their insistence on education, I would not have developed myself this far and taken on the dream of being an educator. Yet that was not enough for me and I decided to be a practitioner and an educator so that I could marry these two worlds together. I am very grateful for that. And thank you to my siblings, especially my sisters, Rita Rai and Sumen Rai, who always watched over me and guided me in life. We played so many creative games in our younger years and I bring some of those experiences in this book. And not forgetting my husband, Kathirasan K, for believing in everything I do and encouraging me to write.

To each and every one who has helped me to get these ideas into writing, THANK YOU.

Foreword

In times of challenge and change, parents and child professionals can feel helpless about finding ways to support their children's development. And yet, no times in history were without such challenges, and still parents found ways to help their children thrive through curiosity, creativity and more.

In our time, Sunita Rai has come up with a wonderful book and approach to help guide our kids through growing up with art, mindfulness, positive psychology and more, all contained in this wonderful book you are holding in your hands. While the world around may be swirling with chaos, in the pages of this book children can discover and reconnect with stillness and strength within themselves and bring that to difficulties they encounter. From compassion and self-compassion, to mindfulness and awareness, acceptance and fun, kids and adults alike can explore so many concepts that most of us never learned until adulthood, if we ever learned them at all. What's more, the book introduces these through creative writing, art and reflection.

I've always believed that the best books for young people speak to both adults and children. While this book has dozens of simple and sweet activities and reflections for kids, when practised with a parent or trusted adult, the benefit doubles and conversations can begin to flow more naturally on topics like peace, good deeds, self-awareness, mindfulness and more, bringing adults and children together more closely as they connect through art, conversation and mindfulness.

In this book you'll find many complex social and emotional concepts and lessons, adapted for younger ages, but without losing depth or impact. And yet, as they grow with this book, and the world changes around them, this book will help kids develop so many of the emotional intelligence skills they'll need for whatever changes the world brings by the time they reach adulthood.

Enjoy!

Dr Christopher Willard

Cambridge, Massachusetts USA
Author, *Growing Up Mindful*
Faculty, Harvard Medical School

Introduction

Hello. Ni hao. Selamat pagi. Vanakkam. Bonjour. Konnichiwa. Hola. Marhaba. Sawasdee Khrap. Namaste. Jambo. Ciao. Anyoung haseyo. Xin Chao. Hallo.

Parents and teachers have spent years developing their children to be agile, resilient and successful. The definition of success differs from parent to parent and teacher to teacher. However, we all agree that we want our children to flourish, to be happy and to be a positive contributor to the world. There is no argument about that.

Today, we face yet another challenge of helping children navigate through the new world of possibilities and complexities. Parents and teachers are the guides through which children learn their role in life, values, academic skills, life skills and social emotional skills amongst others. This learning is all part of their wellbeing. Mindfulness practices contribute toward and enhance children's wellbeing and also that of their parents and educators. A mindful child is like a sponge, always willing to learn and absorb more, and knows what to let go of so that new experiences and skills can be taken in. My aim is to help develop mindful children, together with you, the parents and the educators.

So what is mindfulness? Dr Jon Kabat-Zinn, the father of secular and modern mindfulness, shared that "Mindfulness means paying attention in a particular way: on purpose, in the present moment, and non-judgmentally." It's really about being in the moment with the moment-to-moment experience. Kathirasan K., in his book,

Mindfulness in 8 Days, further elaborated that there are three components to mindfulness: self-awareness, paying attention and practising acceptance. We will be exploring these concepts for children in this book.

How should you use this book?

I would encourage you to use it as a weekly activity book over 25 or 50 weeks. For each of the 25 themes, there are activities, reflections, experiments and mindful colouring. There are no hard and fast rules about how to use the book. Do what works best for your child and you. There are many possibilities for how to use this book. The book is organised such that it starts with something to experiment with or reflect on for the week followed by an image for the child to colour. You could ask your child to colour the artwork first and have a conversation about the value/word etc. Or you could start with the activity and do the colouring at the end of the week as a closure or keep it for the following week. You could also just take a word and talk about it casually using life examples before starting any of the activities. For example, for Peace, you could ask your child why is peace a daily commitment and how it shows in our actions. The idea is to start slow and engage mindfully with your child. Focus on getting into deeper conversations and reflections with your child rather than trying to finish the book. You can in fact spread it over 50 weeks or longer if that works.

How to colour? Encourage your child to engage as many of her senses as possible in the moment, "sense-by-sense". So one way we could start is with the eyes, where you encourage your child to look at the crayons, colour pencils and paints and tell her to make a choice on which she would like to use today and wby she prefers that for today. Maybe she has a reason and maybe not and that's ok.

What are the words written on the packaging or the colour pencil/crayon/paint? What is the packaging like? Using the sense of touch, ask her to feel the packaging and the pencils/crayons. Are they smooth or rough? What else does she notice? Then tell her to perhaps pick five colours that she would like to use for that creative image. Once she has picked them, you can remove the rest of the colours so as to reduce distraction. You could ask her the reasons for choosing the colours if you want. Let her explore if there is any smell on the crayon or colour pencil. And when she starts colouring, ask her if she can focus her attention on the sound that is made while she is colouring. After which, you can tell her to focus on each section as she colours. You could incorporate mindfulness practices between each section if you wish. For example, after she colours for five minutes, you pause with her and focus on your breath for one minute before continuing to colour.

I am excited to explore this journey together. Let's begin our tour with a message to your child.

Note for Teachers
The intention of this book is to weave in mindfulness practices and allied practices into the social-emotional learning (SEL) framework. Research, and my own work with schools, educators and parents, has shown the self-regulatory benefits of mindfulness in improving academic achievements, attention, relationships, emotional regulation, self and social awareness, decision making and behavioural self-regulation amongst others. You could incorporate the concepts within this book into your weekly curriculum to complement the students' learning.

THE JOURNEY BEGINS...
WITH A CLEAR INTENTION

Welcome, my friend. I will be your mindfulness friend for this book. Yes, you have me with you for the next few months working hand-in-hand to be a mindful child.

We will work together just like how it takes two hands to clap. Join me!

I have been travelling with mindfulness for many years and I invite you to join me. Let us tour together in the next few pages and explore the world of mindfulness within you.

You will be on an adventure with mindfulness using this book as a guide to help you through every week. Why? So that you can to get to know your awesome self much better, reduce your stress levels, and become happier and happier and happier. Does this sound exciting for you? Yes!

Before we begin, I have a wish for you. Here it goes:

May you be kind to yourself and others.

May you be compassionate to yourself and others.

May you be loving to yourself and others.

May you be strong.

May you be a positive influence on everyone you meet.

And what is your positive wish for yourself? Fill in your request:

May I be

_____

May I be

_____

May I be

_____

May I be

_____

May I be

_____

Let the journey begin, my friend. Hold on to your pencils, colour pencils, crayons, paints and put on your creative hat and let's go travelling. We shall start with Peace!

PEACE

Peace is a daily commitment.

When we are peaceful inside, we can be peaceful on the outside and with others.

The Peaceful _____ (write your name here) is

an Attractive _____ (write your name here).

    Find a quiet area in your home or class and make it into a peace sanctuary. Whenever you feel like shouting or screaming at someone, choose peace instead. Go over to your peace sanctuary, notice how your body is feeling and focus on your breathing or dance the negative energy off.

What makes you feel peaceful?

Draw your symbol of peace on a piece of paper. You can paste it at your peace sanctuary if you wish.

NOTICE YOUR BODY
Your body is a gift.

You are beautiful as you are. Take a look at yourself in the mirror, and smile at yourself. Be confident about your body. Say thank you to your body every day. It is a gift.

Without your body, how will you play or feel?

Without your body, how will you walk, run, and dance?

Without your body, how will you hug your mom or your dad?

Draw an outline of your body and write the words "thank you" inside.

BREATHE
Your breath is always with you.

How does a blue whale breathe? Go check it out! And do you know, it can absorb 90% of the oxygen that it breathes in, while we humans can only absorb 15%.

Let's practise breathing like a blue whale! Take a deep breath in and balloon your belly (notice your stomach rising) and as you breathe out, notice how your belly flattens. If you want, place a soft toy on your belly and notice it rising and falling as you breathe in and out. Repeat this cycle 5 to 9 times a day, especially when you feel upset, angry or sad. Use your breath to support you in life.

Draw your belly here when you breathe in.

Draw your belly here when you breathe out.

DO GOOD
You are good. You are complete.

People love children who are good. And you make a lot more friends by being a good person. Be positive by seeing the positive in yourself and also in others. Compliment your parents, siblings, friends and also your teachers whenever you can. Always choose to be kind to others. Kind deeds include helping someone on the road or sitting with a friend who is sad or lonely, or holding the door open for others.

What are some good deeds you have done this week? List them here.

1.

2.

3.

What are some good deeds you are going to do next week? List them here.

1. _____
   _____
   _____

2. _____
   _____
   _____

3. _____
   _____
   _____

Do GOOD

GROWTH
Focus on your growth as a person, just like a tree.

What is your dream? Who do you want to be when you grow up? Let's write it down below.

I want to be

1.

2.

3.

Now choose one item from the list above. Choose the one that makes you most happy. What do you need to learn to be that person? What skills do you need? Who can help or support you to achieve it? (You can do this same exercise for the other two items on the list.)

Now visualise yourself being that person. How do you look? What do you see? How does your body feel? What do you feel emotionally? What do you hear? What can you taste, if any? Spend at least 10 minutes or more by closing your eyes and visualising this image, perhaps daily.

GROWTH

SELF-AWARENESS

Discover yourself to be truly happy.

Who are you with 24 hours a day and 7 days a week? Yes you got it right. YOURSELF. So wouldn't it be great to know yourself better? Before knowing others such as our friends, we need to know ourselves well. Let's journey into you.

What are your strengths and areas to enhance?

Strengths	I will be better if I……

What motivates you? Think of two to three examples.

What do you believe in strongly? Think of two to three examples.

LOVE

With love, comes peace and goodness.

Love yourself first so that you can fully love others. Only then can you spread this love around the whole world. Love includes smiling at others, listening to your friends when they are sad, showing respect to your teachers and hugging your parents daily. If you have a pet, love is exactly how you care and play with your pet.

Love is an expression and an action. Write down as many ideas as possible on how you will show love to yourself, your family, friends and teachers. I have added examples in the list below to get you started.

Myself	Love is caring for others as much as you care for yourself.		
	Mother, father and siblings	Friends	Teachers
Smile at myself in the mirror every day.	*Hug all of them.*	*Listen to them when they share their life stories.*	*Greet and smile at my teachers every day.*

OTHER-AWARENESS
Looking through others' lens to enhance happiness.

Are you able to tell what your friends are thinking and feeling? When you can understand your friends better, you form closer and longer-term friendships with them. And you become happier as a result and have more friends to play, laugh and dance with.

Think of a situation when your best friend was sad or angry or happy.

- What made your friend sad/angry/happy?

- What was his or her body language like?

- What was their facial expression?

- What do you think he or she was thinking at that moment?

- What do you think he or she was feeling?

- Was that a positive, negative or neutral feeling?

- How would this feeling have impacted his or her body?

- What did she/he do?

- How do you feel now thinking about this incident?

- How do you think you could have helped your friend in this situation if he/she was sad or angry?

- How do you think you can share in his/her joy?

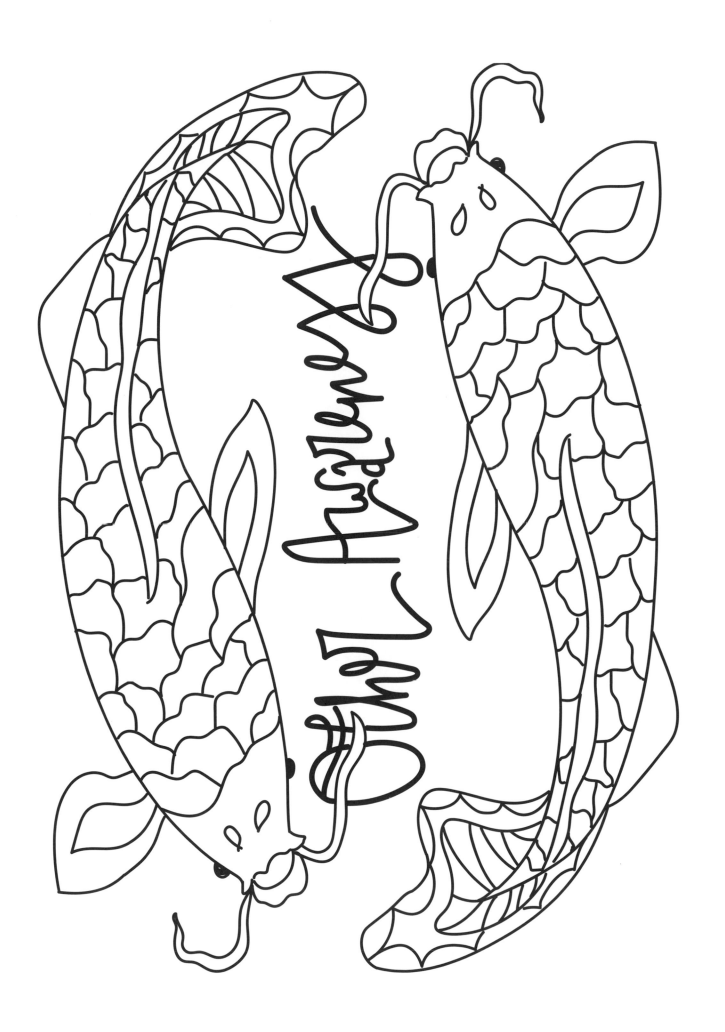

RESILIENCE
Stand up when you fall and embrace difficulties.
Keep going forward.

How many times did you fall before you learnt to walk? Ask your parents to share with you on how you learnt to walk, run or ride a bicycle. Trust me when I say that you definitely fell more than once. And that's okay as that is how we learn.

How many times have you failed in something? That's okay too. Just keep going forward.

How many times have you felt like a failure? That's okay. Hug your failures! Why? Because you are always learning from the mistakes to become a better version of you. Let's write down some of these areas where you didn't do so well and what you learnt from it.

What did I not do well in?	What did I learn from this?
eg. I failed my math test.	Well, now I know that fractions are my weakest topic. I can now focus more on fractions. The teacher's tips on fractions are something I can try out with my next few worksheets.

Start with the ideas listed here.

1. Take positive risks. Come out of your comfort zone and try something new. What will it be today?

2. Ask for help. It's okay not to know everything. Seek help from others and learn to depend on others and allow others to depend on you.

3. Look for the positives in a negative situation. For example, what is a positive thing you can learn when you fail a test?

4. Strengthen your problem solving skill. Find something challenging and sit with it for a few days to solve it. Don't give up.

5. Share your emotions, both positive and negative, with your friends and families. And listen to others when they share theirs.

WISDOM
Be PERRI wise.

Being wise is about **PERRI**:

– **P**ause: Do not react. Pause and breathe.

– **E**motions: Check in with your emotions and those of others.

– **R**eflect: Think about the possible reasons and impact of that situation.

– **I**ntentions: Ensure that your intentions are right.

– **R**espond: Plan what and how you would like to respond using both your head and heart.

Let's try completing the sentences in this table to practise wisdom:

	Wise choice	**NOT a wise choice**
I can learn	*good values from story books, my teachers and parents.*	*how to get others to fear me by learning from the bullies.*
My good friend will		
I should spend money on		
I can show care to others by		
I make decisions by		
I know right from wrong by		
It is important for me to		

	Wise choice	NOT a wise choice
I manage time by		
Every day, I commit to		

BE POSITIVE
Positivity brings out the best in you.

Friends and family love being with people who are positive. They uplift each other's moods.

Now look at your inner voice. Does it say positive things about you? If not, it is time to change the channel and reduce the volume of the negative messages in your mind and increase the volume of the positive messages. You don't need to be perfect, you only need to love yourself as you are.

Change your lens towards a positive lens. Write down the positive and negative voices in your mind in the lenses below.

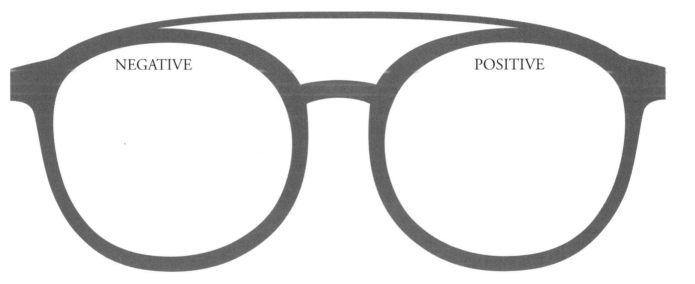

On a daily basis, journal at least three positive emotions for every negative emotion you experience. Remember, the positivity ratio is 3:1. And if you can, also write three positive thoughts for every negative thought that comes into your mind. Start today.

BE POSITIVE

ROSIE

CALM

Stay in the moment.

Can you learn swimming when you are drowning? That might be difficult.

To learn anything, we need to be calm. Stay cool-headed with less noise in your mind by using the Coping Breathing Space practice stated below. Be in the moment and not get trapped in your thoughts about the past or worries and anxieties about the future. Once your mind is calm, you can make PERRI wise decisions.

Let's practise this Coping Breathing Space (CBS) daily for at least three times a day to calm our mind. It's as simple as ABC:

Awareness of your body:

- Pause everything that you are doing. Let it go.

- Bring yourself into the present moment by standing tall like a giraffe and in a comfortable posture. If possible, close your eyes.

- Becoming aware of your body and the surface upon which you are sitting or standing. How does it feel like standing here?

- Notice or mentally scan your body from your feet and all the way to your head.

- Then ask yourself: What am I thinking right now? How am I feeling?

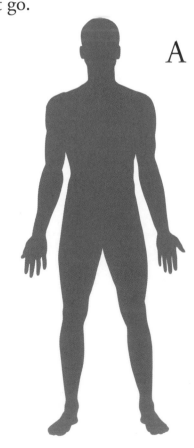

A

36

Focus on your **Breathing**:

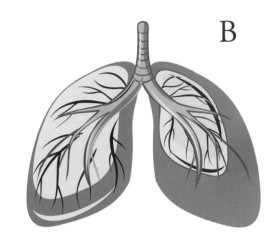

- Now direct your attention to your breathing. Place your right palm on your heart area and the left palm on your belly.

- Follow each in-breath and each out-breath as they follow, one after the other.

- Notice the belly rising and falling with every in-breath and out-breath. Notice how your palm moves along with the breath.

- When the mind wanders, gently guide it back to the breath. Your breath is always with you. Use it to stand firmly or sit comfortable.

Consciously expand your breathing to the whole body:

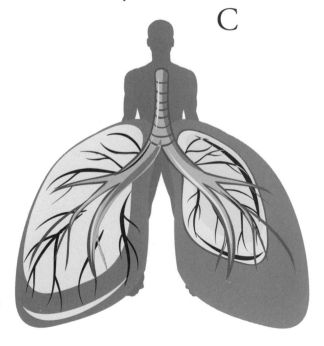

- Expand your awareness around your breathing.

- Let your breath move from your head to your feet by scanning your body and letting the whole body breathe.

- Notice how the entire breathing body feels while it is firmly standing or sitting.

When you're ready, open your eyes and return to your present moment.

BE CREATIVE
Let go so you can explore.

Creativity comes with taking a chance and letting go of perfection. Sometimes we don't try doing new things or play new games because we are afraid of failing or being shamed. But we can't be creative unless we are willing to embrace failure. It's okay to be fearful of failure. It's natural. So give yourself the freedom to fail and freedom to keep trying. Each time you fail, you learn something. So you try again. Try and explore. If you fail again, you try again with a different method. You are always learning. Only then can you see yourself blooming. Let's get rolling.

1. Cook or bake something today with your parents or older sibling and try out some new ingredients.

2. Try out a science experiment with your parents today or perhaps a magic trick.

3. Pick up something. And now think of how you can use it differently. *For example, what else can I do with a colour pencil besides colouring?*

4. When watching a movie or reading a story book, ask yourself how you would end this movie or story differently.

5. Find a space in your home and call it the creative corner (with your parents' permission). Keep all your creative things in this creative corner such as your drawing blocks, materials, colours and others. Whenever you can, sit here and create anything you want. Let's start by giving the creative corner a name and let's create a Creative Hat for you. Draw a design for the Creative Hat in the box on the next page and then make one and leave it in the creative area. Wear this hat whenever you want to create or innovate.

Name: _____ Hat design: _____

MINDFUL EATING
Eat colourful meals everyday.

How do you eat your daily meals? In front of the television or while speaking with your friends? Don't miss out on the colours, flavours, textures and 'sounds' of your food. Eating is a colourful experience if you eat mindfully. Let's try. Now go grab your favourite fruit or any snack. Do clean your hands before you start this practice.

1. Look at your food as if it were food that had arrived from a spaceship. It is alien to you. Imagine it has just dropped from the spaceship and this is the first time you are looking at it. Look at the snack. Notice the shades of colours, lines, grooves, bumps, dents and size.

2. Hold the snack in your palm. How heavy is this snack?

3. Now slowly and gently touch the snack. Feel the texture. Is it smooth or rough? Soft or hard? Hot, warm or cold?

4. Bring the snack closer to your ears and notice any sounds. Press the food gently between your fingers and listen to the sounds or perhaps there is no sound at all.

5. Bring the snack closer to your nose. Smell the snack. What does it smell like?

6. Now place the snack on your tongue, but do not chew it. How does it feel like to have your food on your tongue? Roll it around your mouth. How does it feel?

7. Now take a bite. Notice the juice, flavour and sensations. Take another bite and notice any new flavours.

8. Now as you munch, notice the sound of chewing. Chew the snack at least 10 times.

9. As you swallow, notice the sensations of swallowing your food from your throat and down to your stomach.

10. Continue eating another snack or fruit and repeat the above process.

Do this every day for your first three mouthfuls of every meal. Pay attention to your food.

Have a variety of colours in your food, fruits and snacks for a colourful and happy life. For the next one week, write down all the food and colours of the food you have for lunch or dinner. After one week, ask yourself what colours would you like to add to your meals.

Day	Food	Colours
Monday		
Tuesday		
Wednesday		
Thursday		
Friday		
Saturday		
Sunday		

HUG YOURSELF
Hug yourself to love yourself.

Hugging makes you happier, more cheerful and a lot more loving to yourself and others. And you know, it also releases positive chemicals in your brain and reduces stress. Hug yourself daily, perhaps every morning and night.

Let's learn how to give ourselves a tight hug.
- Open your arms wide and stretch out in front of you.
  Take a deep breath.

- Slowly bring your arms towards your chest and then up towards your shoulders. Continue breathing.

- Press both of your arms into your body as if you are hugging your teddy bear or your pet.

- Hold yourself here for a while, close your eyes and smile.
  You can also rock back and forth slowly if you want.
  Hold on for 10 seconds.

- Now stretch out your arms wide in front of you and repeat again for two more rounds.

How does it feel? Besides the above, what other methods are there for hugging yourself? Be creative and design your own special hug for yourself. It's your 'ME HUG'!

ENGAGE YOUR SENSES
Tap on your FIVE senses to live life fully.

Your five senses are always with you. Engage with your senses in a step-by-step manner to increase your Sense Superpower. By doing so, you can enjoy more of life.

Let's practise together with this practice called Mindful Perception:

- **Touch**: Close your eyes and walk around the house by using your sense of touch. As you touch the items, describe them in detail to your parents or siblings or in your own mind.

- **Smell**: Continue walking around the house and pretend that you are a bear. Try to smell as many things as possible such as your clothes, books, wall, flowers, toys, etc. And notice the difference in each smell. Fun fact: Bears can smell 2,000 times better than humans.

- **Sound**: Now use your elephant ears to listen to the sounds around your home. Listen to the fan, the washing machine or the water running from the tap. Or perhaps when you go to the park or the playground, close your eyes and listen to as many sounds as possible and label them.

- **Eyes**: Now, open your eyes for 30 seconds. Use your samurai eyes to look around the room and memorise what everything looks like. Next, close your eyes and visualise the scene in your mind. And now look again. What did you notice? What did you miss?

- **Taste**: Walk over to your kitchen and take a glass of your favourite drink or milk or perhaps water. Now drink as slowly as you can and focus on the taste. Or eat a snack and chew as slowly as you can like a cow and notice every single taste in your food like you learned in Mindful Eating (page 41).

HONESTY

Build the NEST by being truthful and doing what's right.

Only a strong and courageous person can be honest. Do you agree with me? YES! And you are more lovable when you are honest, truthful and choose to make the right decisions.

So let's build a nest of hoNESTty. Write down your ideas on how you can be honest and show more honesty on a daily basis. Let's start by completing this worksheet.

Tick the statements that show that you are honest.

	HoNEST	DIShonest
I always return things that I find. I never pretend that they are mine.		
I don't fulfil my promises.		
I choose wrong over right as it makes me popular.		
I do not take or steal other people's things.		
I take responsibility for my feelings and actions.		
If I know I will get into trouble for something, I will lie to escape the punishment.		
I do not lie. I always tell the truth.		
I apologise when I make a mistake.		
I do not copy other people's work.		
I do not make excuses for my actions.		

What else will you do to build your hoNESTy?

My hoNESTy

_____

_____

_____

_____

_____

_____

_____

_____

_____

_____

OPENNESS TO EXPERIENCE
Open your mind's door to experiences and happiness.

Your mind is one of your greatest superpowers. Use it. Expand it. Build on it.

Let's experiment together:

- Take a deep breath through your nostrils, then trap the air into your mouth and now open your mouth slightly and push all the air out in multiple directions and let all of your tensions out. Do this 3 to 5 times.

- Pretend that you are an alien or a zombie. Walk slowly around your home and notice how your legs and body move. Notice every single movement, your joints and your muscles.

- Stand like a statue for 2 to 3 minutes. Notice how your body feels when it is not moving and when you remain in that posture.

- Listen to your favourite music and dance away. Create your own dance moves. Then pause after one song and close your eyes. Listen to your heart rate, breath and your body. Now letting go of the body, switch on the music again and listen to all the musical instruments in the song.

- Lie down on your bed or a yoga mat. Close your eyes. And use your "mental eyes" and scan your body (like an X-ray machine) from your feet to your head. How is your body feeling?

What else are you willing to EXPLORE?

My Exploration Adventure

1. _____

_____

_____

2. _____

_____

_____

3. _____

_____

_____

ACCEPT YOUR EMOTIONS AS THEY ARE
Connect with your emotions. Do not reject them.

Activity 1: What do you do when you are ANGRY or SAD?

Your emotions are a guide. They show you what is important to you and what matters to you. There is no need to hide your feelings or to run away from your feelings.

Let's try to ACCEPT our emotions with these steps:

1. If you are feeling angry, sad, mad or irritated, sit down. Yes, sit down.

2. Drink a glass of water if you need to.

3. Label your emotions and say it out: "I am feeling angry!"

4. If you need to cry, go ahead and cry. If you need to shout out in the privacy of your room, shout out.

5. Then close your eyes and befriend this anger or sadness or any other emotion. Say it out loud: "Anger, I accept you. I will sit here with you. I will not fight you. I will sit here with you."

6. And then do Coping Breathing Space (CBS), which can be found under the header of Calm (page 36).

Accept your emotions as they are.

Activity 2:

Befriend your emotions so that they do not have a strong hold over you. Accept them as part of your life. Emotions are not good or bad. They are just emotions. Emotions give you an idea of what is important to you. You need not fight them or fear them. Hug them and accept them. And when you are calmer, reflect on your emotions.

How do you REFLECT on your emotions? Perhaps use a past negative incident to do this.

1. Incident: What happened? Who was there?

2. Name the emotion: What were you feeling? Were you feeling sad, mad, angry, frustrated or disappointed? Let's give this emotion a name. Don't rush through it. Take your time to decide what you were really feeling. Remember it's just an emotion.

3. Action: What did you feel like doing when you were sad or angry or any other emotion? What did you do in this incident? How was your energy level after you had done that?

4. Helpfulness: How did that action help you? Did you feel calmer or more relaxed?

5. Reason: Why did you feel this way? Think of the real reason for being angry or sad.

6. Hurtfulness: Who was hurt in this process? What happened to your relationship with the person?

7. Resolve: How would you like to repair or reconnect with this person? What are you willing to do? How will that help?

8. Future: What can you do in future when something similar happens again? Who can support you in this journey?

PRESENT MOMENT
Dance with the NOW.

When you think of the past or the future, you cannot enjoy the Now. Being in this very moment, the Now, helps us to stay focused and happier, while reducing anxiety and stress.

So let's explore ways to enjoy the moments in our life. Here are some examples:

1. Be bored! Yes, be bored sometimes. Let go of your laptop and smartphone and just sit quietly for 5 to 10 minutes (or longer) a day. You will realise that you become more creative.

2. Paint anything. Do not plan it, just take your brushes and start painting.

3. Play your favourite song and listen to the song with all your attention. You can also dance with all your energy to the song.

4. Draw something and focus on your drawing such as the strokes, shapes, etc. as you do it.

5. Close your eyes and listen to your heartbeat if you can. You can also focus on your breathing.

6. Do your stretches and focus on all the muscles and joints as you move, moment to moment.

7. Scan your body and notice how your body is feeling right now.

8. Use your spoon or fork to gently hit on things around you and listen to the sounds they make.

What else can you do to focus on the Now?

PRESENT MOMENT

FUN

Be silly, have fun, play more and rewire your brain.

Did you know that you can wire your brain towards positivity by having fun? Try anything new from today such as walking a new route when going home. Let's try a few fun activities together.

1. Frog jump: Stand up. Place you right palm on your heart area and your left palm on your belly. Notice your heart rate and how your body is breathing right now. And now let go of your hands and start jumping like a frog for 1 minute. And then pause. Now place you right palm on your heart area and your left palm on your belly. Notice how your heart rate has increased and how your body is breathing right now. Pay attention to how your body has changed and how it slowly relaxes.

2. Reach for your toes: Sit on the floor and stretch out your legs. Now slowly use your fingers to crawl all the way to your toes. And stay here for a few seconds. How are your back, stomach, legs and hands feeling right now? Now slowly, using your fingers, crawl back to the original position. How is your body feeling right now?

3. Zombie walk: Walk around the room like a zombie. How is your body feeling? Which part of your body is uncomfortable? Now, raise your right hand towards the sky and keep it still and continue walking like a zombie except do not move your right hand. How does it feel to not move one part of your body while moving the rest?

4. Cloud connection: Walk out to your garden or the playground. Lie down on the grass or ground and look up at the sky. Now count all the clouds that your eyes can see. Now look at only one cloud. Try and see what it reminds you of. Is it like a car or building or aeroplane?

5. Now create three fun things to do on your own. The only rule is that you must fully engage with the activity by paying attention to it.

My Exploration Adventure

1. _____
   _____
   _____

2. _____
   _____
   _____

3. _____
   _____
   _____

COMMITMENT
Do things daily for your happiness.

Commitment is easy. You agree to do ONE thing every day that benefits your family, your friends, your teachers, the society and YOU. For example, you commit to practising honesty every day. Let's make some commitments today by completing the sentences below:

1. I will help my mother/father/grandparent

   _____.

2. I will exercise for _____ minutes thrice a week by doing

   _____.

3. I will learn

   _____.

4. I will clean

   _____.

5. Every day, I will smile at

   _____.

6. When I am angry, I will

   _____to calm down.

7. I will practise mindfulness every day for _____minutes.

Now create three more commitments on your own.

My Commitments

WORDS CREATE OUR WORLDS
Your words can heal the world.

What do you prefer to hear: the good or the bad? What do you think others would love to hear: the good or the bad?

Your words are very powerful. Be mindful of how you use words. Use them with care and love. The words in your mind and when you speak should make you feel good about yourself and helps others feel good about themselves.

WORDS means:

- **W**arm: Smile and be warm and cheerful in conversations. Show care and concern for your family, friends, teachers and others.

- **O**pen: Be willing to explore in conversations. Allow the other party to share their views and explore all possibilities. There are always two sides to a story.

- **R**espectful: Respect others by not interrupting them and being kind and gentle when you respond. Treat everyone the way you would like to be treated.

- **D**ependable: Do what you say so that people can trust you. Never break promises.

- **S**incere: Be truthful, honest and genuine when talking to others. If you are unsure, ask questions to clarify. When you make a mistake, be willing to apologise.

What words are helpful and what words are hurtful?

HELPFUL	HURTFUL

CREATIVITY

Flow through your imagination to create.

You are naturally creative. Mindfulness helps you to enhance your creativity. Let your imagination run wild and explore your dreams. What is something that you have always wanted to explore or create but have not yet done it?

Let's explore some creative ideas and remember not to judge yourself in the process. We are interested to only explore and the idea is not to be perfect. Be compassionate to yourself with whatever results you get.

1. Doodle daily. Notice every stroke you make as you doodle.

2. Write your own poem using your own life experiences. Now read the poem out loud and write down your emotions and thoughts about this poem as if you were hearing it for the first time.

3. Write your own lyrics and music and sing it to you family. How do you feel hearing yourself sing?

4. Take one item of your clothing and convert it to something else, such a pencil case, wrapper, etc. What did you create? How do you feel about it?

5. Change one thing in your bedroom to make your room look different from before. It can be something small or big. How do you like your room now?

Let's try something together. I have done the first stroke in the box opposite and I would like you to help me complete the picture by continuing the drawing. There is no right or wrong. I will love anything that you have drawn as it is uniquely you.

EMOTIONAL INTELLIGENCE
*Connect with your head and your heart
to be successful in life.*

Which is more important: to think with your head or with your emotions? Or is it both? Emotional intelligence is the ability to use both your head and your heart to make decisions. This includes:

1. Self-awareness: What are you thinking right now? How are you feeling? What are some of your strengths? What are some areas for you to improve? What do you value? What motivates you? Check out more in the topic of Self-awareness (page 24).

2. Other-awareness: Think of one of your buddies. Now think of any incident that was not pleasant where either of you felt angry or upset. What was your buddy thinking at that time? How was he or she feeling? What are some of your buddy's strengths? What are some areas for your buddy to improve on? What does your buddy value? What motivates your buddy? Use some of the strategies under the topic of Other-awareness (page 28).

3. Self-regulation: How can you manage your feelings when you feel angry or upset? Try the practices in Breathe (page 18) and in Calm (page 36). Accept your emotions as they are (page 52).

4. Social Skills: How do you connect with your friends? Try smiling more often and finding good things to say about your friends. Of course you need to be sincere. Notice their strengths and perhaps share with them what strengths you see in them. And help them when they are in need. Go out with them and play together. Or sit down and have conversations about games, families, school, movies and others. Friends are important in life and you need social skills to stay connected.

What else can you do to enhance your emotional intelligence?
List down three more ideas.

1. _____
_____
_____

2. _____
_____
_____

3. _____
_____
_____

EMOTIONAL

INTELLIGENCE

THE JOURNEY CONTINUES...

Well done, my friend. You have completed your long journey of being with yourself and learning mindfulness.

I have a wish for you for the rest of your journey. Here it goes:

May you be well.

May you be happy.

May you be healthy.

May you be at peace.

May you be a positive influence on the whole world.

And what is your wish for the world? Fill in your request:

May the world be

_____

_____

_____

May the world be

_____

_____

_____

May the world be

_____

_____

_____

May the world be

_____

_____

_____

May the world be

_____

_____

_____

Thank you for journeying with me and may your journey with YOU be bright and cheerful.

ABOUT THE AUTHOR

Sunita Rai (PsyD) is a skilled mindfulness teacher, wellbeing coach, psychotherapist, counselling and psychology lecturer and supervisor. She is the Executive Director at Centre for Mindfulness and the Managing Director at Holistic Psychotherapy Centre. She holds a doctorate in psychology and researches on the impact of mindfulness on children and adults.

BY THE SAME AUTHOR

Mindfulness for the Family
A parent-child workbook for greater awareness and stronger relationships

Written for parents of kids aged 5–12, this fun and wise book brings families together through the art of mindfulness. Most people think of mindfulness as a solitary pursuit, but in fact the aim of mindfulness is greater acceptance and compassion for others. This workbook offers a wealth of specially designed activities for parents and children to practise mindfulness together – in the home and outdoors. For parents who are stressed about raising "perfect" children, and for kids who are experiencing "growing pains", mindfulness has proven benefits. Let this book be your guide.